Pre-twentieth Century
Short Stories
A Teacher's Resource Book

Jean Moore and John Catron

Hodder & Stoughton

A MEMBER OF THE HODDER HEADLINE GROUP

Acknowledgements

Illustrations: Chris Blythe pp 11, 13, 33, 41, 48, 49, 52

Orders: please contact Bookpoint Ltd, 39 Milton Park, Abingdon, Oxon OX14 4TD. Telephone: (44) 01235 400414, Fax: (44) 01235 400454. Lines are open from 9.00 – 6.00, Monday to Saturday, with a 24 hour message answering service. Email address: orders@bookpoint.co.uk

British Library Cataloguing in Publication Data
A catalogue record for this title is available from the British Library

ISBN 0 340 73743 3

First published 1999

Impression number   10 9 8 7 6 5 4 3 2 1
Year   2004 2003 2002 2001 2000 1999

Copyright © 1999 by Jean Moore and John Catron

Cover photo: Duntroon Castle, Argyllshire, © Marsden Archive/Bridgemann Art Library
Typeset by Fakenham Photosetting Limited, Fakenham, Norfolk
Printed in Great Britain for Hodder & Stoughton Educational, a division of Hodder Headline Plc, 338 Euston Road, London NW1 3BH by Hobbs the Printers, Totton, Hampshire.

CONTENTS

INTRODUCTION

This publication, together with a Student's Anthology, has been specifically designed to meet the needs of English teachers in relation to the National Curriculum requirements for pre-twentieth century texts. The anthology is a collection of seven stories which represent some of the most gripping and intriguing narratives of this period. There are many fruitful links between the stories and yet they cover between them a diversity of universally relevant themes. The combination of vivid settings, mysterious plot and fascinating characters ensures that they will be well-received by secondary students.

This Teacher's Book contains a wide variety of strategies – oral work, active reading, drama and written responses – designed to make the stories accessible for readers in both Key Stage 3 and 4.

Using the Student's Anthology and the Teacher's Book

The Student's Anthology contains a brief introduction to each author and a stimulus page. It has long been accepted that in order for students to begin to engage with complex and, at times, archaic narrative text, it is necessary to do some or all of the following:

- stimulate their interest and curiosity in the setting, characters or themes
- provide glimpses of connections between their world and the world of the story
- make students active inquirers into the background of the story through researching information
- pose questions which intrigue or puzzle
- establish a pattern of understanding from which they can launch their own reading.

The double page spread utilises these ideas and provides an initial link between the reader and the text.

The Teacher's Book provides a summary of strategies and a rationale for their use on the first four pages devoted to each short story. This can be used as a planning device by teachers or simply as background material. The final eight pages in each section are in the form of photocopiable pages designed to assist reading and reflection on the text.

Helping Students' Understanding

Although these are short stories, the progress of the narrative may still appear to be lengthy for less experienced readers. They may, therefore, require activities during their reading which continue to stimulate their interest or strategies which cause them to pause in their reading and to reflect. These include:

- enlarged text
- dramatisation
- labelling
- imaging or picturing.

Enlarged Text

Students often find the complicated syntax and vocabulary daunting in pre-twentieth century texts. The sheer volume of 'difficult' words on the page can be initially off-putting. The purpose of enlarging the text, with space surrounding it, is to make the text appear more accessible to inexperienced readers. Space between and around the words can then be used by students to mark, underline, be active with the text and so become more at ease with its cadences.

Dramatisation

Again, inexperienced readers sometimes require the ephemeral process of reading – picturing the story in the 'mind's eye' – to be made tangible and concrete through dramatisation. By choosing two volunteers who can be directed by the other members of the class to enact the movements and words of the two characters, students are able to externalise the process of reading. The physical presence of the two characters enables students to see, touch, perceive and act upon them and to use the text and make sense of it.

Labelling

The process of slowing down reading is important to allow students to become more familiar with the rhythms and structures of pre-twentieth century text; it allows them to 'get the hang of it'. Labelling pictures requires students to skim read to locate specific information and then place the chosen quotation next to the relevant section of the picture, thus linking image and meaning.

Imaging or Picturing

A number of activities consist of students engaging in imaginative exercises which use text as stimulus for art work. Such creative responses to reading help to fix students' understanding and to validate what may be quite individualistic illustrations.

These activity pages can be used discretely or as a coherent approach to a single story. They also contain pages which encourage written response and comparison with other texts. Post-reading activities are often associated with assessment in the form of lengthier written pieces as analysis or comparisons. Consequently, the pattern of activities in all of the short stories asks students to either reflect on crucial aspects or themes in the story, to write creatively in diary or in letter form or to analyse aspects of the story with a view to making a direct comparison with another text of their choice.

To assist students in locating crucial passages, there is a system of icons in the margin to direct them to the precise point in the text where they will need to focus their attention. For example:

(The number refers to the relevant page in the Teacher's Resource Book.)

Story Summaries

In this introduction each of the seven stories is also covered in a brief overview to allow teachers to remind themselves quickly of the plot and to assist planning.

Themes and Subject Matter

This introduction contains a guide to the themes and subject matter of each story so that teachers can make informed choices about which texts to teach in comparison to other texts they are studying with groups.

COMPARATIVE TEXTS

The following books are suggested as possible texts for comparative work.

De La Mare, W., 'The Wharf' in *Modern Short Stories* (ed. J. Hunter). Faber and Faber.

Hill, S., 'The Badness Within Him' in *Frankie Mae and Other Stories*. Hodder & Stoughton.

King, S., 'The Body' in *The Four Seasons*. Hodder & Stoughton.

Lawrence, D. H., 'The Rocking Horse Winner' in *Love Among the Haystacks*. Penguin.

Lawrence, D. H., 'The Horse Dealers' Daughter' in *The Second Penguin Book of English Short Stories* (ed C. Dolley). Penguin.

Lively, P., 'The Darkness Out There' in *Frankie Mae and Other Stories*. Hodder & Stoughton.

O'Brian, P., 'Samphire' in *Modern Short Stories* (ed. J. Hunter). Faber and Faber.

STORY SUMMARIES

1 *The Signalman* by Charles Dickens

The famous short story of a troubled man, isolated in his place of work and haunted by a figure warning him of death. His tale is gradually told to the narrator but ends with his own death on the railway line.

2 *The Dream Woman* by Wilkie Collins

The story of Isaac is told to a doctor by the landlord of a country inn. It is a tale of ill-luck, a terrifying dream, an unsuccessful marriage to a woman that Isaac comes to believe had haunted him in the dream, and his fear that she will find him again.

3 *The Withered Arm* by Thomas Hardy

This story deals with a rejected woman, Rhoda, and her eventual friendship with her ex-lover's new wife, Gertrude. Immediately after Rhoda's dream of Gertrude struggling with her, Gertrude's arm begins to wither and her marriage to farmer Lodge begins to fail. Desperation leads Gertrude to seek help by touching the neck of a hanged man. But he is discovered to be the son of Rhoda and Farmer Lodge, and the shock is too much for her.

4 *The Monkey's Paw* by W. W. Jacobs

Three wishes are offered by the visitor to an ordinary family using the strange talisman.

But the first causes tragedy, and the second horror. Can the third wish save them?

5 *The Black Veil* by Charles Dickens

This is the story of a mysterious visitor seeking help from a doctor. But the instructions she gives are strange and enigmatic. He travels to her desolate house, to find a dead body brought upstairs to a bedroom. It is her son, hanged that morning.

6 *The Melancholy Hussar* by Thomas Hardy

Phyllis lives in an isolated cottage with her morose father. When Humphrey Gould makes an offer of marriage, it seems a sensible choice and an opportunity for change. But he does not return to marry her, she meets the homesick soldier, Matthäus and falls in love. Her plans of happiness are cruelly thwarted by fate and her concern to do her duty.

7 *The Yellow Wallpaper* by Charlotte Perkins Gilman

The fascinating account of a woman's innermost thoughts and gradual detachment from reality when a rest in the country is recommended. As she loses control over her life, she becomes obsessed with the wallpaper in her room, and the woman she believes is trapped behind it.

THEMES AND SUBJECT MATTER

Story	Theme
The Signalman	isolation
	gothic/mystery
	premonitions
	ghostly apparitions
The Dream Woman	isolation
	love and loss
	mother/son
	premonitions/dreams
The Withered Arm	prejudice
	justice/punishment
	evil/superstition
	the status and role of women
	mother/son
	loss
	fate
	isolation
	marriage
The Monkey's Paw	mother/son
	loss
	desire
	the supernatural
	fate
	three wishes
The Black Veil	sorrow/loss
	justice/punishment
	violent death
	mother's love
	madness
The Melancholy Hussar	isolation
	love
	justice/punishment
	loss
	duty
	fate
	women's choices
The Yellow Wallpaper	isolation
	illness
	marriage
	madness
	ghosts/visions
	power and lack of it

THE SIGNALMAN

by Charles Dickens

Stimulus Page

Use the stimulus page in the Student's Anthology to begin to stimulate interest in and curiosity about *The Signalman*, prior to reading.

Picture This...

Use the extract on page 8 of the Student's Anthology to close read, annotate and dramatise the opening to the story.

This specific piece of enlarged text deals with the very first, significant action and dialogue in the story. It is important to focus closely on it because it contains an enigma which can be used to further intrigue the reader: the fact that the signalman reacts to the call from this visitor in exactly the opposite manner to that which we might expect. At the sound of 'Halloa! Below there!' he looks straight toward the tunnel mouth and not towards the direction of the noise. The reason why he reacts like this is unravelled as the story progresses.

- Suggest that the students work in pairs to use the space around the words to highlight, underline and annotate the text as they clarify the positions of the characters.
- Decide whether to dramatise the extract by working in small groups or as a whole class.
- Stimulate discussion and prediction about the signalman's reaction to the visitor's call and what it might mean. You may want students to record these initial responses in their file.

Down the Zigzag Path

Use the picture on page 11 of this book as a guide to select specific quotes that relate to the setting of the story.

With the picture of the tunnel and cutting in front of them, students are able to select relevant information from the text and place it in the appropriate position. As an activity, students are learning to select and use quotes at the same time as they are slowing down the process of reading to consider short phrases in more depth.

- There are several alternatives for the re-reading of this section: pairs or small groups for able readers, as a whole group with the teacher reading for mixed groups. There is an added possibility of asking

students to close their eyes and listen to the vivid descriptions.
- The annotations given should help the students to choose appropriate quotations.

The Sense of Foreboding

Refer to the worksheet on page 12 of this book. Ask students to use the space on the sheet to collect specific examples of vocabulary.

This activity will be useful to help students realise the connection between words and atmosphere. If students are encouraged to perform this activity at regular intervals, it will enable them to grasp aspects of style and grammar and gradually become more critical readers.

- An appropriate point to start might be after the first conversation between the signalman and the visitor.
- An alternative approach would be to ask the class to work in groups and to divide the text from the description of the cutting to the end of the first conversation into small, roughly equal sections. Less able readers could then be directed to a smaller section of text whilst having the support of a partner.

Conversations

Use page 13 of this book to summarise the important information gained from the dialogue between the two characters.

A considerable amount of interesting background information on the signalman can be gleaned from these sections. It may be necessary to return to it at a later date but for students to do this, they first need to grasp the basic outline of the story the signalman relates to the reader. The page can then be used as a starting point for the hot-seat drama exercise on page 14.

- Ask students to work in small groups and to make a list of the five most important points to emerge from each of the two conversations.
- As a whole group, discuss which are the final five you can all agree upon.
- Some weaker readers may need specific passages outlined in advance to help them focus on the text. Working with a partner or within a supportive group might also help.

THE SIGNALMAN

by Charles Dickens

States of Mind

Use page 14 of this book to dramatically explore the signalman's state of mind.

Having summarised the two conversations between the signalman and the visitor, students need to explore the deeper issues which they reveal about the signalman's dilemma. Drama provides a context for close questioning and consideration of a character's feelings, background and mental state. It may be necessary for the teacher to take on the role of the signalman to control the drama but a confident and experienced student would be equally appropriate, or a combination of both.

- Using the summary of the conversations from the previous exercise, ask students to work in groups to identify six questions which they feel are crucial to understand the signalman's behaviour at this point. Allow a short period of say five minutes for this brainstorm activity. (It might be possible to use this activity as an assessment session for oral work and thereby add a further element of tension to the work.)
- When the students are ready, set up the classroom according to the diagram on the worksheet with students keeping to their groups and asking questions in turn.
- Any notes taken by students could be placed on sugar paper and shared by the group as background notes for the psychologist's report.

Railways Board Report

Use page 15 to produce a report into the death of the signalman, commissioned by the Railways Board.

A useful piece of coursework would be for students to write down their understanding of the signalman's state of mind in the style of a report. The previous drama work will have helped prepare students by providing them with a clearer insight into his psychological health.

- The specific requirements of each sub-heading will need to be fully explained; the observable evidence section contains the facts, the diagnosis the opinions.
- Students will need to be encouraged to use a style which is appropriate to the formality and seriousness of the report.
- The word list will need to be defined and used in context by asking students to create one formal sentence each, place it on sugar paper and display it around the room.
- This page acts as preliminary notes and could lead to either a full report covering several pages or an analytical essay covering the character of the signalman.

Seeing the Story as a Whole

Use the selected quotes on page 16 of this book and rearrange them to form a summary of the story.

Students are now approaching the stage in the story when they need to be able to have an overview of the essential points so that they can begin more in-depth, reflective work. This page provides a sequencing task which will result in students having a simple summary to use with the remainder of the work on this text. It would be a suitable preparation for many pieces of coursework.

- Students will need the text of the story and their other notes alongside them in order to make decisions.
- The activity could be done individually or in pairs.
- It is important for students to use their own words on the A3 summary sheet so that they are clarifying for themselves the significant points in the story.
- When they write about why each piece is important they will need to be directed towards a consideration of structure, meaning and reader response, for example, the revelation of the signalman's feelings is important because it creates sympathy in the mind of the reader.

Making Comparisons

Use the columns on page 27 of this book to compare specific aspects of two different texts as a basis for a coursework assignment.

This Dickens short story is a good example of his style and art and a comparison with another author and time can lead to surprising and illuminating revelations about how literature works. This page offers a way into making comparisons between texts, firstly in note form backed up by quotes, and, secondly in paragraphs backed up by an assignment.

- The meaning of the word 'theme' needs to be fully explored so that students go beyond the idea of simple messages to the deeper underlying and universal themes of texts such as in films, adverts, poems and even cartoons.
- Possible themes for comparisons:

Theme	Also found in
mystery/gothic	*Dracula* by B. Stoker *Jekell and Hyde* by R. L. Stevenson
darkness	*The Darkness Out There* by P. Lively
premonitions	*The Rocking Horse Winner* by D. H. Lawrence *The Dream Woman* by W. Collins

THE SIGNALMAN

By Charles Dickens

Picture This ...

In order to begin to understand a story, it is sometimes necessary to spend some time looking closely at a short extract to find out exactly who the characters are and what they are doing. *The Signalman* is an eerie story set in a very strange place; so, we need to picture it ...

In small groups, or as a whole class:

① Read the extract once again before you begin.

② Look for particular words that act as 'stage directions', telling you exactly how the two characters speak and move. Highlight these. Look for the examples which have already been done for you before you add others.

③ Choose two volunteers from your group to be the signalman and the visitor. The rest of you need to annotate the text so that you can act as directors of a short scene guiding the two volunteers as they move and speak exactly as the two characters in the story. The annotation given will guide you.

④ Within a circle, place these two characters in the positions they occupy at the start of the extract. Which way are they facing, who speaks at which moment, what are the differences in height?

⑤ As the two volunteers dramatise the extract, using the actual words and movements of the characters, what is puzzling about the way the signalman reacts?

'Halloa! Below there!'

When he heard a voice thus calling to him, **he was standing at the door of his box**, with a flag in his hand, furled round its short pole. One would have thought, considering the nature of the ground, that he could not have doubted from what quarter the voice came; but instead of looking up to where I stood on the top of the steep cutting nearly over his head, he turned himself about, and looked down the line. **There was something remarkable in his manner** of doing so, though I could not have said for my life what. But I know it was remarkable enough to attract my notice, even though his figure was foreshortened and shadowed, down in the deep trench, and mine was high above him, so steeped in the glow of an angry sunset that I had shaded my eyes with my hand before I saw him at all.

'Halloa! Below!'

From looking down the line, he turned himself about again, and, raising his eyes, saw my figure high above him.

THE SIGNALMAN

By Charles Dickens

Down the Zigzag Path

clammy stone

the zig-zag descent

The setting of the story, where it takes place, is very important to the mood and atmosphere. The cutting where the signalman works seems to affect the way he thinks and behaves.

① In pairs or small groups, read from 'The cutting was extremely deep … as if I had left the natural world.'

② Find as many descriptions of the setting as you can and underline them.

③ Write these short quotations next to the illustration above so that you have an actual quote for as many parts of the illustration as possible. You might use this for display.

THE SIGNALMAN

By Charles Dickens

The Sense of Foreboding

What words or short phrases can you find to write on this page? Note down words that Dickens has used to create a sense of foreboding. Try to find hints of the supernatural; the dark side of human experience; a suggestion of unpleasantness and the unexpected.

THE SIGNALMAN

By Charles Dickens

Conversations

The visitor goes to see the signalman on two occasions during the story. On each occasion he learns something new about him.

① The first is at the very beginning of the story until the two say goodnight. Go back to this passage and, in pairs or small groups, find four or five important facts that the visitor learns about the signalman, his job and his past life. Jot them down in the bubble marked 'Visit 1'.

② The second visit begins with the line 'Punctual to my appointment ...' to ... 'he would not hear of it.' This time the visitor learns about the accidents and the apparitions which the signalman says that he sees. Skim through this section and find the ten key pieces of information to write in the bubble marked 'Visit 2'.

THE SIGNALMAN

By Charles Dickens

States of Mind

You will need to refer to your notes from the Conversations sheet, page 13; to help you with this activity.

The signalman is a complex character who is beset by problems. Some problems are from his background and others seem to have been caused by working in the gloomy isolation of the cutting.

Is he a diligent but sane person simply trying to do his best or is he a disturbed personality who should not be working in a position of responsibility?

The visitor makes the following statements about the signalman as he attempts to understand him:

- the monstrous thought came into my mind … that this was a spirit, not a man

- I have speculated since whether there may have been infection in his mind

- I should have set this man down as one of the safest of men to be employed in that capacity but when I saw him in this state, I saw that for the poor man's sake, as well as for public safety, what I had to do for the time was to compose his mind

By using drama, you can begin to probe deeper into the mind of the signalman and decide for yourself about his state of mind.

① Read through your notes made on the conversations between the signalman and the visitor.

② Consider the comments listed above made by the visitor about the signalman.

③ Now, working in a group, assume that you have been employed by the Railways Board to gather evidence about the signalman which might explain the events. Jot down a list of six essential questions which you will put to the visitor.

④ Ask one member of the class to be the visitor and to take on that role in a hot seat. The volunteer may want another person to support them in this role so that they can quietly confer before giving a response to your questions.

⑤ Allow each group to ask one question at a time and nominate a small group of people to take notes so that they can be used later by the whole class.

THE SIGNALMAN

By Charles Dickens

Railways Board Report

You are going to prepare a report into the death of the signalman. The report has been commissioned by the Railways Board.

A Report into the Death of the Signalman

Make up your own Railway Board insignia.

Purposes of Report

- To establish the state of mind of the signalman prior to his death.

- To decide on ways to prevent a re-occurrence of the tragedy.

Observable Evidence

- He answered all my questions clearly and directly.

-

-

Diagnosis

- He seemed an intelligent and honest man.

-

-

Recommendations

- The Railways Board should consider employing two men on each night shift.

-

-

-

Useful Vocabulary

- diligent
- professional
- introspective
- loyal
- frustrated
- unstable
- concerned
- depressed
- lonely
- lucid
- vigilant

THE SIGNALMAN

By Charles Dickens

Seeing the Story as a Whole

① Now that you have finished your initial reading, it is important to be able to understand the story as a whole. One way to do this is to organise the quotes on this page into the correct order so that you have a brief summary of the essential moments. Cut them out and arrange them correctly.

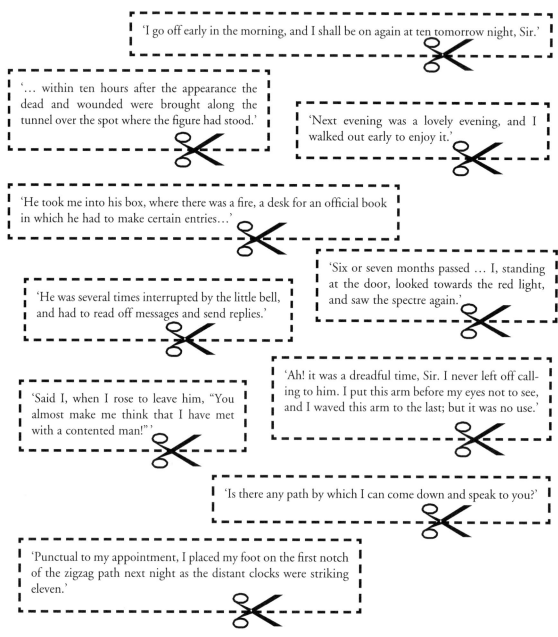

'I go off early in the morning, and I shall be on again at ten tomorrow night, Sir.'

'… within ten hours after the appearance the dead and wounded were brought along the tunnel over the spot where the figure had stood.'

'Next evening was a lovely evening, and I walked out early to enjoy it.'

'He took me into his box, where there was a fire, a desk for an official book in which he had to make certain entries…'

'Six or seven months passed … I, standing at the door, looked towards the red light, and saw the spectre again.'

'He was several times interrupted by the little bell, and had to read off messages and send replies.'

'Ah! it was a dreadful time, Sir. I never left off calling to him. I put this arm before my eyes not to see, and I waved this arm to the last; but it was no use.'

'Said I, when I rose to leave him, "You almost make me think that I have met with a contented man!"'

'Is there any path by which I can come down and speak to you?'

'Punctual to my appointment, I placed my foot on the first notch of the zigzag path next night as the distant clocks were striking eleven.'

② Now stick the quotes onto a new sheet of A3 leaving space between each one. In this space write down in your own words which point in the story the quote is from and why you think it is an important moment.

THE SIGNALMAN

By Charles Dickens

Making Comparisons

You can use this passage as a planning sheet to help you plan and structure your Wide Reading coursework assignment.

The Signalman	Other Text	Points to Remember
Setting: • dark, depressing railway cutting near mouth of black tunnel • sides of cutting are steep and wet • signal box is in lonely isolated position •	**Setting:**	**Look for:** • similarities and differences between the two stories. For example, a similar isolated character; a very different outcome
Quotes: • '…as solitary and dismal a place as I ever saw' • •	**Quotes:**	• things you can learn about the writers from these similarities and differences.
Characters: • signalman is intelligent, brooding, isolated • has monotonous but responsible job • is troubled by a recurring vision •	**Characters:**	**For your coursework assignment:** • Use an introduction which clearly states what you will explain fully in the rest of your assignment. • Be sure to stick to the question. • Try to link your paragraphs in a varied way to avoid repeating yourself. Here are some suggestions:
Quotes: • '…educated…but had run wild, misused his opportunities, gone down, and never risen again.' • •	**Quotes:**	One way in which these two stories are similar.… Another point of comparison between the two stories is.… Each of the stories deals with … in a similar way Perhaps the main common feature is.…
Plot: • narrator story is made up of three visits • • •	**Plot:**	• Always try to use evidence to back up a point you are making. Your evidence could be a direct quote or you could simply refer to an episode in the story.
Quotes: • • •	**Quotes:**	• Use a conclusion to sum up, in brief, what you have already explained.
Themes (the major issues in a story): Human isolation — how people can become unstable through loneliness Premonitions — Darkness —	**Themes:**	

THE DREAM WOMAN

By Wilkie Collins

Stimulus Page

Use the stimulus page in the Student's Anthology to begin to stimulate interest in, and curiosity about, *The Dream Woman*, prior to reading.

The questions in this section can be dealt with in a variety of ways: whole class discussion, pair work which is then reported to the class as a whole, or small group work, where one member volunteers to record ideas and these are then displayed or explained verbally. Some questions could be used for individual work, where answers are jotted down for homework, or in a quiet, reflective session in the classroom.

The Story Within

Use page 21 of this book to record the major events of Isaac's story by summarising them, either as the story is read, or afterwards.

This activity provides a way of summarising the major stages of the plot, and helps students to fix the order of these events in their minds. The final sheet is also useful when the story is used in subsequent activities, as it is quick to read and shows the structure clearly. The written work from the activities that follow could all be made into a collection in student files, as evidence of literary response, and as a resource that will enhance the final assignment.

- Brainstorm with the class some of the various ways of structuring a story: for example, chronological, flash-back, jumping from one period in time to another. Many film techniques provide useful examples here.
- When the first section is read, or after finishing the story, the sheet can be used to illustrate the idea of the 'story within'. As students complete the summary points, they will need to distinguish between major changes in the plot, and minor ones. Rough drafts of lists of events could be used before they decide on the sections they believe are the important ones to summarise the story.

Beginnings

Use page 22 of this book to consider the importance of the opening pages in story writing, and study the way Collins creates his beginning.

Again, this work will be relevant later if students create their own piece of original writing. The gathering of ideas here, highlights the importance of past reading experience, and the way in which all readers use this when they approach a new story. The activity is designed to encourage students to be critical and analytical, by stating their 'requirements' for a good beginning.

- Examples of a variety of different well-known stories and films will be useful when the brainstorming session is beginning.
- The decisions reached could be presented on sugar paper, to be referred to and used later.
- The search for examples from Collins's story would be best done in pairs or small groups, so that a small amount of text is studied by each individual.

Painting Pictures

Use page 23 of this book for a study of the language and parts of speech used to create descriptive passages.

These extracts have been chosen as examples of descriptive writing, and will be useful if students do some creative writing of their own. The language analysis is useful for many aspects of both Language and Literature, Key Stage 3 and 4, as it is designed to clarify the way the different parts of speech work in the sentences, and what they add to the text.

- Allow a fair amount of time for the students to study the top extract and its annotations. This could be done individually, with each one jotting down what they now recognise as an adjective, and what a noun. Their own made-up examples will be useful to check understanding.
- As they tackle the second extract, ask them to look for the way the 'pictures' are created by the writer, and the way detail is added. Adjectives are sure to be a part of this!
- It might be useful to consider what categories of description are used: is there an emphasis on colour? form? texture or shape? Coloured pens could be used to analyse these aspects.

THE DREAM WOMAN

By Wilkie Collins

A Mother's Role

Page 24 of this book provides a character study of Mrs Scatchard, Isaac's Mother.

This activity breaks down the idea of a character study into workable sections on which to focus. It could be usefully combined with some drama work, to enable students to explore Mrs Scatchard's thoughts and motivation. It is important to draw out some understanding of her attitude to her son, his dream and his marriage.

- At points in the story stop and ask students to work in pairs. One will take the role of the Mother, and one a questioner, someone who tries to find out what she is thinking. It will be interesting to see whether the words that emerge all show her in a positive light! Read aloud specific points in the story where her more possessive side is shown to extend the responses.
- The sheet can be filled in after this activity, perhaps asking students to record their observations quietly, straight after the drama.
- The comments column is asking students to reflect on what they have written and to draw conclusions: for example, 'She seems to me to be...'

Creating Rebecca

Page 25 of this book enables students to study one character and the attitude of the writer to her.

It is important to use opportunities to deepen understanding of the writer's point of view, his concerns and attitudes. This type of activity is designed to help with this process, as it takes a rather controversial figure and asks students to identify both the positives and the negatives about the way she is portrayed. This is then followed by a piece of imaginative writing where the students decide on the angle they wish to take, using the writing process in a similar way.

- The TB icons at the side of the text in the anthology indicate some of the points where Rebecca is described. Refer students to these, and arrange for them to be read aloud, perhaps more than once, to create the sound of Collins's writing about Rebecca in the classroom.
- The sheet will need to be explained by filling in the first examples as a whole class.
- After some time has elapsed, and students have focused on the textual clues, use a hot-seating exercise to bring Rebecca to life, and deepen understanding. Depending on experience and confidence, volunteers or

the teacher could be used. Ask the person in role as Rebecca to decide on whether they are going to present her in a positive or negative light, but to keep their decision secret. The class asks questions of her, either as a whole or in small groups after some planning time. The second volunteer then takes over, to present the opposite angle. It may well be that there will be a mixture of responses to these questions, quite rightly!

Rebecca's Story

Page 26 of this book helps students to create a piece of imaginative writing in the first person, revealing Rebecca's point of view, thoughts, feeling and motivation.

This follows on from the previous activities. It needs to be carefully focused, or it becomes 'just another diary'. The sheet offers direction and asks students to choose their point of view and to work out how to gain the required response in their readers.

- Provide 'real readers'! Pair individuals from the beginning, to act as critics who will describe their response to the character that emerges from the writing: 'When you describe how she suffered before meeting Isaac, I feel really sorry for her...' 'That bit where you have her planning and scheming makes her seem so cruel and heartless...'
- The use of language will be enhanced by reading aloud Rebecca's words from the text, and by highlighting the more archaic uses of language.
- Decisions about what to include need to be made before writing anything. Allow time for the students to list the topics they wish to include, and encourage the use of appropriate new material that is only hinted at in the text itself.

Making Comparisons

Page 27 allows students to compare the use of dreams and visions in three of the stories from the anthology.

This comparative work asks the students to consider one specific aspect of the stories, in order to make a useful and perhaps more straightforward comparison. Discussion work will be used before the completion of the sheet, and additional sheets of paper will be needed after the columns are filled in.

THE DREAM WOMAN

By Wilkie Collins

- Begin by referring to the original questions on the Student's Anthology stimulus page – 'Do you believe that dreams can foretell the future? Can they directly affect people's lives?' Ask for a period of reflection on this before anyone speaks, so that considered responses are encouraged. Each individual could be asked to respond, by speaking to the person next to them before any whole class discussion takes place.
- After reading the stories, the sheet can be completed, in groups of three perhaps, with each member being responsible for reporting on one story. Discussion and writing can then follow to bring out the similarities and the differences, and to consider what these tell us about the individual writers and the aims of each story.

Your Own Writing

Page 28 of this book provides an opportunity for original writing using some of the ideas or subject matter of these stories.

The study of language, character, plot and writer's intentions in this unit should help students to create their own stories or pieces of descriptive writing. Encourage them to refer back to the sheets they have completed, and to use their understanding of how these stories work to frame their own.

- The quotations at the top of the sheet are best used by asking each student to read them individually, then have them read aloud and any difficulties explained, before discussion takes place. They are designed to stimulate different responses of agreement and disagreement, so this could be a small group activity where ticks and crosses are added to the sheet as they agree on a common response.
- Gathering ideas should be done at the point where the students seem most involved and interested in the theme and its possibilities. Further instructions and advice can be given later, but it is important to let ideas flow, even if they are abandoned or modified later.
- At some point advice and help will be needed so that the common pitfalls and errors are avoided. Examples of previous students' work are useful to show effective beginnings, or repetitive vocabulary, as long as names are removed to protect the innocent!
- Allow time for drafting and modifying, with help from 'a critical friend' who listens to parts of the story as they emerge.

THE DREAM WOMAN

By Wilkie Collins

The Story Within

The Doctor's Story

- He goes to a nearby town.
- He goes to an inn to find cheaper transport.

Isaac's Story

- •
- •

- •
- •

- •
- •

- •
- •

- •
- •

- •
- •

- He hears the last part of the story.
- He asks the final question.

THE DREAM WOMAN

By Wilkie Collins

Beginnings

Stories need good beginnings. What do you think a writer must do at the start of a story? Some ideas are printed below. Add three more, and then search the beginning of this story for examples of how the writer is doing this.

Making it seem real, as if it actually happened:	Making the reader curious about something:
Creating a mood or an atmosphere:	

THE DREAM WOMAN

By Wilkie Collins

Painting Pictures

Study the extract below, and look at the way the techniques used have been highlighted.
What do these words add to the writing? What effect is created?

> Isaac locked the door, set his candle on the chest of drawers, and **wearily**
> got ready for bed. The <u>bleak</u> autumn wind was still blowing, and the
> <u>solemn</u> <u>surging</u> moan of it in the wood was <u>dreary</u> and <u>awful</u> to hear
> through the night-silence. Isaac felt strangely <u>wakeful</u>. He resolved, as he
> lay down in bed, to keep the candle alight until he began to grow <u>sleepy</u>
> for there was something <u>unendurably depressing</u> in the bare idea of lying
> <u>awake in the</u> darkness listening to the <u>dismal</u>, <u>ceaseless</u> moan of the
> wind in the wood.

alliteration 'wind ... wood'

Now look at the second extract, and highlight and annotate it yourself. See if you can spot
the most effective words and phrases and name the part of speech used.

> His eyes fixed on her arm and hand, as she slowly drew her knife out of
> the bed. A white, well-shaped arm, with a pretty down lying lightly over
> the fair skin. A delicate, lady's hand, with the crowning beauty of a pink
> flush under and round the finger-nails.
>
> She drew the knife out, and passed back again slowly to the foot of the
> bed; stopped there for a moment looking at him; then came on – still
> speechless, still with no expression on the beautiful face, still with no
> sound following the stealthy foot-falls – came on to the right side of the
> bed where he now lay.

THE DREAM WOMAN

By Wilkie Collins

A Mother's Role

Mrs Scatchard

What she says and does:	What she is like:	My comments and conclusions:

Add to these columns as you read through the story.

THE DREAM WOMAN

By Wilkie Collins

Creating Rebecca

Rebecca's character is gradually revealed to the reader. How did Collins want us to judge her, do you think? Did he want us to feel sympathy for her, or to be critical of her? Use the columns below to jot down examples from the text that create sympathy or criticism. Look for the way she is described, what she does and says, what is said about her.

🙂 Sympathy	🙁 Criticism

So what is your conclusion? Is Collins painting a positive or negative picture?

THE DREAM WOMAN

By Wilkie Collins

Rebecca's Story

Now you have studied the way Collins presents Rebecca, you have an opportunity to create her again for yourself. Imagine some papers are found one day and passed to Isaac. They contain Rebecca's own writing, describing her view of what happened. What thoughts might be revealed in these documents? You are going to write them, pretending you are Rebecca.

① First, decide what you wish to be the response of your readers. You are in charge! You can make them feel sympathy, or make them criticise Rebecca's actions and schemes, or perhaps a mixture of both.

② Make your first notes below. In the first box, list the parts of her life you have decided to include. For example, will you include anything about her life before she met Isaac? Would this be useful to gain sympathy for her, or would it show a negative side?

Notes

③ Then write down three sample sentences in the second box. Remember to use the first person: 'I can recall the day vividly…he struck me, yes, he struck me.' Try to use words that sound right for the time this is set and the person who is writing: 'I had but ninepence to my name, enough only for a night's lodging. He offered me a new existence. Only a fool would have rejected him.'

Sample Sentences

THE DREAM WOMAN

By Wilkie Collins

Making Comparisons

The three stories named in the columns all have dreams or visions in them. This acitivity helps you to examine how the author uses dreams and visions and what effect they have on the people in the stories. You will need to think about the following questions, before you write your ideas in each column.

● What is seen in the dream or vision?

● Does anything in it seem evil?

● What is the reaction of the character?

● Is there evidence of anything supernatural?

● What effect does it have on the events that follow?

The Dream Woman	The Withered Arm	The Signalman
The figure seems to threaten violence.	Gertrude's arm starts to wither after the dream.	The vision disappears, as if it is supernatural.

THE DREAM WOMAN

By Wilkie Collins

Your Own Writing

Dreams and visions have been the subject of stories for centuries. Below are some statements that might help you gather ideas for your own writing.

'Negative emotions…fear…hatred, anger, or malice…are the guarantee that visionary experience, if and when it comes, shall be appalling.' A. Huxley.

'…I talk of dreams, which are the children of an idle brain…' Mercutio, in Shakespeare's *Romeo and Juliet.*

'Dreams are simply the unconscious mind dealing with or distorting reality.'

'…stories of the supernatural – born of superstition, the fear of death, and our childlike terror of the dark.' H. D. Thomson.

'In the dark of the night the shadow-goer came stalking…' A translation of part of *Beowolf*, probably the first 'ghost' story ever to be written in the language that became English.

Remember! For good writing:

- Create a great beginning (you have completed a Beginnings worksheet)

- Use descriptive writing (remind yourself of the work you did for the Painting Pictures worksheet)

- Plan the ending carefully.

Arrange quotes around a spider diagram:

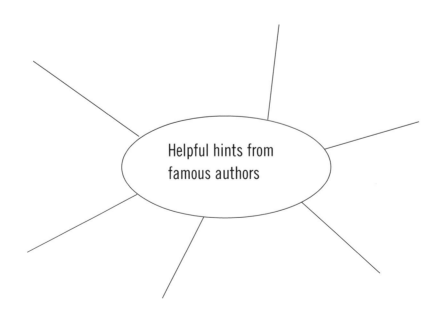

Helpful hints from famous authors

THE WITHERED ARM

By Thomas Hardy

Stimulus Page

Use the stimulus page in the Student's Anthology to stimulate interest in and curiosity about *The Withered Arm* prior to reading.

The questions posed could be used as part of a class discussion, or research could be done independently, ideas and conclusions being written up in files or on sugar paper.

The Village Gossips

Use page 31 of this book to gather information from a close reading of the text.

This activity encourages students to search for clues as soon as the story begins, and to understand key pieces of information that will be useful as they read the remainder of the story. It is also a study of the language used by characters and provides the basis for the play-writing on page 32.

- The actual words spoken by the farmhands could be read aloud to start the activity.
- The tasks could be completed independently, observations then being compared with a partner in the class.

Making a Play

Page 32 of this book provides a script-writing activity based on the gossip of the farmhands.

This sheet reminds students about the layout of a script and then suggests ideas for content. It could be used at a number of points during the reading of the story, as clearly there are many opportunities for village gossip as the events unfold.

- Using the top of the sheet, remind students how to set out a script on the page.
- The activity works best in small groups, so that as the script is written it can be read aloud by the various voices, and modified.
- Several copies will be needed, by photocopying or asking students to make a copy each. The plays can then be rehearsed and performed for the class.

Steps to Tragedy

Page 33 of this book provides a study of the specific causes of the tragedy for three main characters.

This worksheet can be used for a number of texts at GCSE level – from Shakespeare to *Lord of the Flies*. The design appeals to students, and the notes recorded go further than a mere summary by asking them to consider what decisions were made, and what aspects of a character's personality made them take a certain route.

- Begin by discussing one decision that was made by one character, as an example – what influenced them? Personality? Past events? Other people? Personal desires or emotions?
- The task could be done in groups of six, so that two people work on one character, or it could be done in a smaller group which discusses all three together.

Making Drama Out of Tragedy

Use page 34 of this book for a dramatic recreation of the story with fragments of dialogue description and the thoughts of characters.

Students enjoy recreating the story in their own way, deciding what is important and what can be omitted. The activity enables them both to summarise and to create, and the final presentation is usually a unique dramatic collage of words and sounds, revealing much about the story.

- The groups will need to be encouraged to choose carefully. How can the story be told with so few words? What might the thoughts be of certain characters at the key points?
- The sheet will be needed for the first planning activities, and then students will have to jot down further ideas as rehearsals progress.

The Moral Maze and Moral Judgements

Pages 35 and 36 of this book provide a focused discussion about the story and its meaning.

Using this format for discussion encourages students to consider motivation, meaning, the writer's intentions and their own responses. They will also need to justify personal decisions to others and try to reach a compromise if the group does not agree.

- The two pages provide an activity that can be distributed to groups, or even the class as a whole seated in a circle, so that the teacher's role becomes that of observer. It may be necessary to intervene at

THE WITHERED ARM

By Thomas Hardy

points to enable less confident members to voice their views, or to encourage more detailed expression of reasons why they agree or disagree.

- There are opportunities for the assessment of speaking and listening here, so it would be useful to discuss with students what skills will be needed and remind them of assessment criteria. A period of self-assessment would be a useful conclusion for each individual student.
- The statements are best left to the students to decipher and discuss, rather than beginning with a session that explains each word. Groups will need dictionaries and will need to be asked to decide on the meaning of the statement before they decide whether they agree with it or not.
- A plenary session to see whether each group reached similar or different conclusions would be useful at the end.
- This format allows students to explore their levels of agreement on many different issues from the meaning of the story as a whole, to characters, plot and struc- ture. This page could therefore be used at other points in this unit of work, or as a stimulus for discussion about aspects of other stories in this anthology.

Making Comparisons 1

Page 37 of this book is a coursework assignment that asks the students to compare an aspect of *The Withered Arm* to the same theme in another text.

The themes of isolation and loneliness are common ones in literature, and provide a useful focus for comparison. Other Hardy novels or short stories could be used, Steinbeck's *Of Mice and Men*, and even the island aspect of *Lord of the Flies*, where the consequences of being cut off from society are so tragic. D. H. Lawrence's *The Horse Dealer's Daughter* also provides an interesting contrast to *The Withered Arm*, as it does to other Hardy short stories.

- A discussion about types of isolation (physical, environmental, emotional, for example) would be a useful introduction, as would some consideration of the meaning of loneliness and the difference between being alone and feeling lonely.
- Use the sheet to help students to organise their findings and pose themselves the key questions: what are the facts, the reasons, and the effects?
- As they begin writing their ideas into essay form, some help with paragraphs may be needed. The sheet on page 38 will be useful at this point.

Making Comparisons 2

Page 38 of this book is an activity that suggests another theme to explore across two texts, and offers ways into an assignment.

Several stories in this anthology reveal ideas about what has been considered to be 'evil': superstition; supernatural occurrences that seem to defy the laws of nature; human emotions that have been called 'the deadly sins'; cruelty and neglect; the terrible effects of poverty and hardship. An examination of this theme can lead to very interesting discussions about what students now believe 'evil' to be, and the different ways it is explored and revealed through literature.

- Encourage discussion about the above issues by setting up small groups and asking each of them different questions. They should write their responses onto sugar paper, for display, so that these sheets can act as a prompt when they report back to the class.
- Use the six boxes to help students to record ideas, remaining in their groups initially.
- The ideas should then be expanded by each student working alone, gathering further examples, reasons and effects.
- As they begin to write, some students may be able to take the topic further by considering what each writer is saying about evil, and what this reveals about the society and culture of their time.

THE WITHERED ARM

By Thomas Hardy

The Village Gossips

The story of *The Withered Arm* begins with the local people gossiping about the main characters. It is an interesting way to find out about the characters but, as readers, we need to pick up the clues carefully.

① Work in pairs or small groups and read through the first two pages of the story again.

② As you read, underline in pencil any comments which you think tell you something about another character. You may just get a hint of some juicy titbits. These are very valuable.

③ In the first column of the table jot down what you think are the most interesting or important gossipy comments.

④ In the space in the middle column, write what you think you have learnt about the characters.

⑤ In the right hand column, write down what you notice about the way people used language. (Two examples have been done for you.)

Gossip in the farmyard	What have you learnt about the characters	The language they used
'He do bring home his bride tomorrow.'	someone has been married and returns tomorrow	they use the word 'do' differently
'Years younger than he they say.'	the man is a lot older than his new wife	they use 'he' instead of the word 'him'

THE WITHERED ARM

By Thomas Hardy

Making a Play

Imagine that the villagers or farmhands have other opportunities for gossip, as the story of Rhoda and Gertrude unfolds. What might they have said about snippets of gossip they have heard?

① Working in a small group, use what you have learnt about the way these people might talk to write a short scene from a play about the villagers' discussion and their views of the three main characters in the story: Farmer Lodge, his new wife Gertrude and the milkmaid, Rhoda Brook.

② You can use as many farmhands as you like. You might hint at what has happened to the farmer and his wife, or perhaps exaggerate, as gossips often do.

③ Some farmhands might sympathise with Farmer Lodge, others might disapprove. What criticisms would they make, what would their attitudes be towards the married couple and to Rhoda who is, after all, one of them?

Remember how to set out a script. The example below shows how to do this.

Farmhand 1:   _____ ?
Farmhand 2:   (puzzled) _____ !
Farmhand 3:   (walking towards them) _____
    _____

Remember! No speech marks are needed, but other punctuation is important. Separate the names from the words spoken by using a clear margin. You can write it in the box below.

④ Use your script to rehearse and dramatise the village gossip about Farmer Lodge, his new wife and Rhoda Brook.

THE WITHERED ARM

By Thomas Hardy

Steps to Tragedy

Now that you have read the story, it is time to consider the steps which lead each character to their doom.

① Skim back through the story and decide on six or seven crucial factors in the story which helped send your character along the road to tragedy.

② Use the pathways below to record these so that your whole group has a clear idea of the steps for each of the three characters.

Her jealousy

The fact that the hanged man was Rhoda's son

His rejection of Rhoda

THE WITHERED ARM

By Thomas Hardy

Making Drama Out of Tragedy

The Crowd at the hanging

'Eee, imagine if it was your son…'
'I've heard things about his mother, though…'

The judge sentencing Rhoda's son

Farmer Lodge rejecting Rhoda before the story begins

Farmer Lodge writing his will

Gertrude consulting Conjuror Trendle

Rhoda and Gertrude meeting

① Prepare a dramatic presentation of the story made up from fragments of dialogue or the characters' thoughts and pictures of events. Use the Steps to Tragedy sheet on page 33 as a guide to deciding which moments to choose

② Draw pictures on this page to capture some of the actual words spoken in the tense moments of the story or imagine what the characters were thinking or writing.

③ Present the story summary to another group or the whole class, as a dramatic collage which orally captures the atmosphere and tension.

THE WITHERED ARM

By Thomas Hardy

The Moral Maze

Strongly Agree	Agree
Disagree	**Strongly Disagree**

① Work in groups of about three or four. Look at the Moral Judgements sheet on page 36, discuss them and decide in which quadrant you would place them.

② When you have made your decisions, write the statement in the appropriate box.

THE WITHERED ARM

By Thomas Hardy

Moral Judgements

Write these statements in the Moral Maze:

- Farmer Lodge was really responsible for all the tragedies which occurred.

- The story is essentially about jealousy and its effects on people.

- There is no hope in the story. It is totally bleak and pessimistic.

- Hardy believed women had no power or control over their lives.

- Gertrude, as a character, is far too gullible and naive.

- The superstitions are unrealistic and nothing like this could ever happen.

- Rhoda Brook should have recovered from her relationship with Farmer Lodge long before Gertrude arrived.

- For Gertrude to accidentally go to Rhoda's son's hanging is too much of a coincidence to believe.

THE WITHERED ARM

By Thomas Hardy

Making Comparisons 1

This page is designed to help you plan a coursework assignment. The title for this assignment is:

Compare the isolation and loneliness of the characters in *The Withered Arm* and a text of your choice.

The Withered Arm	Other Text
Facts Rhoda's cottage is outside The village	
Reasons The villages' prejudice against her Her pride	
Effects She has few friends	

① Think of as many ways as you can in which the characters in *The Withered Arm* are isolated or lonely. Write these down in the 'Facts' box.

② Discuss why these characters are so isolated. Write your reasons in the 'Reasons' box. Then decode on the effects of this, and record your conclusions in the 'Effects' box.

③ With a new sheet, repeat the process for another text you have read.

④ For each of the facts try to find a quote to justify or pack-up what you are saying.

⑤ Are there similarities or differences between the isolation and loneliness of the characters in the two stories?

⑥ Begin writing your assignment.

THE WITHERED ARM

By Thomas Hardy

Making Comparisons 2

A theme is an issue at the heart of a narrative text. The theme you are to consider for this comparative coursework assignment is that of 'evil'. Your assignment is:

Compare the theme of evil in *The Withered Arm* with its treatment in another narrative text of your choice.

The Withered Arm	Other Text
Examples	
Reasons	
Effects	

① In *The Withered Arm* what actions or thoughts would you describe as evil? Write this list in the 'Examples' box.

② After you have read your text, make a similar list on the right hand side of the page.

③ What similarities and/or differences do you notice?

THE MONKEY'S PAW

By W. W. Jacobs

Stimulus Page

Use the stimulus page in the Student's Anthology to begin to stimulate interest in and curiosity about *The Monkey's Paw* prior to reading.

These pre-reading activities are designed to link with students' own reading experience and to provide some background research and information. The picture itself contains clues to add to the process of speculation and prediction. For instance, the spare chair by the fire suggests the arrival of a visitor.

The Chess Match

Use the opening section of the story and page 41 of this book to close read, annotate and gather insights into the three main characters.

It is important for students to have a clear understanding of not only the setting, which they gain from the picture, but also the characters and their relationship to each other, if they are to draw conclusions about their respective attitudes to the concept of 'fate'. The opening paragraphs up to the arrival of Sergeant-Major Morris, contain subtle insights into the characters' personalities.

- Ask students to re-read this opening section in pairs or small groups to focus their attention on the characters.
- Suggest the use of pencil to underline significant or revealing comments.
- Share the insights made so that the whole group has a secure framework to proceed in the reading.

Stop and Think 1 and 2

Use pages 42 and 43 of this book **during the first reading of the story**. Students should say what will happen next and give their reasons from the text.

As with many short stories, *The Monkey's Paw*'s success depends on the vague yet growing sense of impending tragedy built up in the reader's mind. Tapping into this unease can help students to clarify their responses and to reflect upon them at the end of the story. Prediction develops skills of inference and, when shared with the whole group, can help inexperienced readers to pick up on clues in the text.

- At the suggested points in the story, stop the reading and ask the students to turn to this sheet.
- Briefly discuss what has occurred in the story to that point and, working in pairs, ask students to use that

knowledge to predict what will happen next.

- As you move on in the reading, take time to occasionally look back at predictions – not to decide who was right or wrong but to verify predictions and to acknowledge the possibility for alternative structures.

Looking at Words

Use page 44 of this book to collect 'difficult' vocabulary so that a bank of words and definitions supports the reading.

Archaic or complex vocabulary can inhibit young readers when they encounter pre-twentieth century texts. By acknowledging this complexity and providing open, structured means of dealing with them, it is possible to remove many of the misgivings students feel when they encounter these words.

- Explain to students that such words are included in the text and that their initial overawed reactions are perfectly normal.
- Make the exercise something of a playful inquiry and challenge students to find as many 'really difficult' words as they can. Use dictionaries or provide definitions yourself to assist in the 'demystifying' process.
- Encourage students to explore the words further by asking questions about their usage. Explain how words become archaic and ask students to make their own judgements on whether words are currently in use.

Drama and Reading

Use page 45 of this book to enact and discuss the various interpretations and to reflect on the concept of 'fate'.

Bringing a piece of written text to life in the form of a scripted performance adds not only motivation to reading but also a variety of insights as different groups interpret text in subtly different ways.

- It may be necessary to acquire the use of a drama room or to re-organise the room so that space is available for rehearsal and performance.
- Set a time limit on the exercise and ask students to be creative in their interpretations of the text.
- Stress that different approaches are welcomed and use these differences to reflect on the original text and the different ways in which students have 'read' the story.
- In the box at the bottom of the page, ask students to write in their understanding of the father's and mother's view of fate. Their view is also required as a link to the activity on page 46.

THE MONKEY'S PAW

By W. W. Jacobs

Being Alfred Hitchcock

Use page 46 of this book as a script so that students read the original text and translate it into a dramatic script.

Media transfer is an active method of reading which involves students in altering a piece of text so that it is appropriate for use in another medium. In this case, students are asked to transfer prose into script form. This involves them in close reading of the original, annotation of the 'new' script and an awareness of the changed audience and purpose of the piece.

- Ask students to read the original prose text and to identify the speakers on the script sheet.
- By underlining the emotive words in the original and transferring them as stage directions, students will gain an understanding of how their scripts should be performed.
- Performance readings are best done in the security of pairs and fours but some, more confident students may wish to offer their interpretation to the whole group for discussion.

Wording Wishes

Use page 47 of this book to focus students' attention on writing sentences which are precise in their meaning.

This page draws on students' knowledge of the convention of 'three wishes' in narratives and on the slippery nature of 'meaning' in language. It is a playful challenge which students enjoy meeting.

- Discuss the wishes Mr White makes and speculate on what his final wish might have been.
- Challenge students to come up with a form of words which could circumvent the fakir's view that fate could not be changed and that it was dangerous to attempt it. Ask them to write the wishes in such a way that tragedy could be avoided. Discuss their attempts.
- Place them in the fakir's role and, after swapping the re-written wishes, ask them to find a way to make the outcome into a tragic one.
- As an extension, try asking them to write their own three wishes in a way which could avoid the fakir's tragic predictions.
- It may be possible to enter into a discussion about fate and whether students believe in life as being pre-ordained. This links to the expression of their views on page 45.

Mrs White's Keepsakes

Use page 48 of this book to generate ideas for writing in a variety of forms in response to the story.

Making writing 'real' is an accepted way of giving students a purpose which provides motivation and a linguistic challenge. This page extends the story by assuming a box of documents is discovered in the attic and asking students to imagine what it might contain. Some students may need further assistance with this but others may well think of a wide variety of items to include.

- Talk to the group about Mrs White and how she might react to the death of Herbert. What sort of things would she be likely to keep? Ask students to write their ideas on the box lid and to share them with the rest of the class. It may be necessary to explain some legal documents and terminology.
- Have plenty of card, blank paper and felt pens for students to make whatever documents they think are appropriate.
- Use the resulting documents to make a display of 'real' writing responses to *The Monkey's Paw*.

Receiving the News

Use page 49 of this book to focus closely on some extended written pieces for coursework.

Students may well have generated many ideas on page 48 but coursework requirements, and the development of writing skills, demand that some pieces be more detailed and extensive. Two of the exemplar pieces on this page demand high level writing skills so that the vocabulary and sentence structure strike the appropriate tone. One is a public piece of writing; the other is more private.

- Find some newspaper cuttings and bring them into class as examples of how tragic news is written in newspapers.
- Use the outline for all students but some may wish to work independently to review the story and write it up, others may need to be directed to the section and to be given paragraph headings to help them along.
- The bereavement letter might require a list of appropriate words and phrases on the board or on display, which students can 'stitch together' to create the letter.
- The death certificate can be used by less able students or as an indicator to all about what is required by law under such circumstances.

THE MONKEY'S PAW

By W. W. Jacobs

The Chess Match

Discovery Box: Herbert
Discovery Box: Mrs White
Discovery Box: Mr White

As you read through the opening sections of *The Monkey's Paw* you will pick up clues about Mr and Mrs White and their son, Herbert. The story begins in the White's isolated cottage with father and son playing chess and mother knitting by the fire.

In small groups or pairs:

① Re-read the opening section when the family are waiting for the arrival of their visitor, Sergeant-Major Morris.

② Look carefully at what happens during the chess match. What is Mr White trying to do in the game? Which of the two wins? Without looking, Mrs White seems to know what is going on. How can she know this?

③ As you pick up clues about the characters, write what you have learnt in the appropriate 'Discovery Box'. You may want to share your findings with the whole class.

④ As you read on in the story, you may wish to return to this page and add some more brief points about these characters.

THE MONKEY'S PAW

By W. W. Jacobs

Stop and Think 1

The Monkey's Paw is considered to be a great story because, as readers, we are never really sure what will happen next. The story gives us so many tantalising possibilities. On this page, you are asked to stop at three different points during your reading of the story and predict what you think might happen next and why you think that will happen.

Working in your pairs or in small groups:

① On page 84 of the Student's Anthology, Mr White makes his first wish and he cries out because the paw seems to move in his hand. Herbert and Mrs White run towards him. What do you think will happen next? Why? Write your predictions and reasons in the table on sheet 2, page 43.

② On page 86 of the Student's Anthology, a second visitor arrives at the cottage who, at first, is very quiet. Why do you think he has come and why do you think that? Write your predictions and reasons in the table on sheet 2.

③ On page 90 of the Student's Anthology, Mrs White can't reach the door bolt. Will she open the door, and, if so, what will she find? Write your predictions and reasons in the table on sheet 2.

THE MONKEY'S PAW

By W. W. Jacobs

Stop and Think 2

What happens	p 84 Herbert and Mrs White run towards Mr White	p 86 A visitor arrives who is strangely silent	p 90 Mrs White can't reach the door bolt
What might happen next?			
Why do you think this?			

THE MONKEY'S PAW

By W. W. Jacobs

Looking at Words

One of the reasons for reading pre-twentieth century stories is that they provide us with such a rich variety of words which we can then use ourselves in our own writing. A list has already been started for you with some definitions on the right hand side. When you have found a word, try to find out whether it is still in use today. If so, put a tick in the middle column. If it is not in use place a cross.

Word	In use?	What it means
Amiably	√	in a friendly way
Condole	√	express sympathy
Rubicund	x	red-faced

① As you read the story, underline in pencil any words that you want to add to your vocabulary list and write them in the left hand column.

② Use a dictionary to find out what they mean and write in the definition.

③ Ask your teacher or another adult if they use the words. If they do, the word is in use today and you place a tick in the middle column. If it isn't commonly known, place a cross.

THE MONKEY'S PAW

By W. W. Jacobs

Drama and Reading

① Work in pairs and find the section of the story in the Student's Anthology (page 87) which begins: 'It was about a week after...' and ends with '...walked to the window and raised the blind.'

② Using the script on page 46 write on which lines belong to the mother (M) and which to the father (F).

③ Re-read the extract and write onto the script what the character is doing and how they should say the lines. (In the actual story, there are plenty of clues such as, 'The paw!' she cried wildly.)

④ Still working in pairs, choose who wants to be the father and who the mother. Bring the scene to life by rehearsing it, using the movements and emotions you have written onto the page.

⑤ Show your work to another pair and watch theirs in turn. Compare the two versions. What have you done the same and what differences are there? You may wish to perform your scene for the whole class.

This scene is about people's belief in fate — whether our lives are already planned out for us by a higher force. The fakir wanted to show that fate did rule peoples' lives. What do the characters think?

⑥ Write in the spaces below what you believe the three main characters thought about fate. Is it foolish and wicked to try to change fate?

Mother's view:	
Father's view:	
Your view:	

THE MONKEY'S PAW

By W. W. Jacobs

Being Alfred Hitchcock

'Come back ... You will be cold'

'It is colder for my son'

'The paw! The monkey's paw!'

'Where? Where is it? What's the matter?'

'I want it. You've not destroyed it?'

'It's in the parlour, on the bracket. Why?'

'I only just thought of it ... why didn't I think of it before? Why didn't you think of it?'

'Think of what?'

'The other two wishes ... we've only had one.'

'Was that not enough?'

'No ... we'll have one more. Go down and get it quickly, and wish our boy alive again.'

'Good God, you are mad!'

'Get it ... get it quickly, and wish – Oh, my boy, my boy!'

'Get back to bed ... you don't know what you are saying.'

'We had the first wish granted, why not the second?'

'A coincidence.'

'Go and get it and wish.'

'He has been dead ten days, and besides he – I would not tell you else, but – I could only recognise him by his clothing. If he was too terrible for you to see, how now?'

'Bring him back ... do you think I fear the child I have nursed?'

'Wish!'

'It is foolish and wicked.'

'Wish!'

'I wish my son alive again.'

THE MONKEY'S PAW

By W. W. Jacobs

Wording Wishes

It could be said that Mr and Mrs White's mistake was to word their first two wishes without planning and thinking.

① Work on your own or in pairs.

② Look carefully at the wishes Mr White makes. Can you think of three better wishes which would not have been so tragic for the White family? Write them in the space on the right hand side of the table.

The actual wishes	Your re-wording of the wishes
I wish for £200	
I wish my son alive again	
What did Mr White actually say?	

③ Swap your re-worded wishes with a partner. Read theirs carefully. If you were the fakir, how would you make their wishes turn out tragically?

④ If you had the monkey's paw yourself, what wishes would you make and how would you word them so that they brought you happiness?

-
-
-

THE MONKEY'S PAW

By W. W. Jacobs

Mrs White's Keepsakes

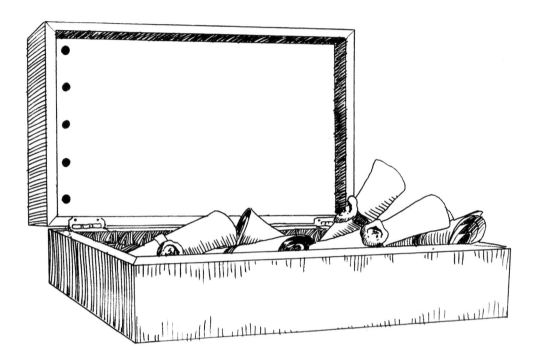

Mrs White was obviously a devoted mother and Herbert's death was a terrible blow for her. In the attic of the cottage, she kept a box which contained many papers, documents and memories of Herbert.

① Working with a partner, think of as many different documents, papers or other things which Mrs White might keep to remind her of her son. Write this list in the space provided on the box lid.

② You are going to make some of these documents. Some of them will be quite simple (for example an old theatre ticket) and some will be more complicated (perhaps a letter Herbert sent whilst on holiday). From your list on the box lid, make as many documents or memorabilia of Herbert as you can. You may want to display some of these.

THE MONKEY'S PAW

By W. W. Jacobs

Receiving the News

Three particular documents which Mrs White has kept are outlined on this page. They are: a cutting from the local newspaper, the letter from Herbert's employers and his death certificate.

On a separate sheet of paper, it is your job to complete the documents.

You will need to consider the following:

① The Newspaper. What headline would you use? How would the newspaper describe Herbert's death?

② The Death Certificate. What are the essential details which would need to be included?

③ The Letter. This is a very difficult and sad incident. How would the company write about his death?

THE BLACK VEIL

By Charles Dickens

Stimulus Page

Use the stimulus page in the Student's Anthology to begin to stimulate interest in, and curiosity about, *The Black Veil* prior to reading.

The Lonely Doctor

Use page 52 of this book to focus on the setting of the story and on the doctor's situation.

Many stories in this genre begin with similar elements. This page is designed to highlight these features and to provide an insight for students into the character and situation of the doctor. The picture itself begins the process of imaging which students themselves are asked to develop as the activity progresses.

- Tell the class that imaging comes from vivid selections in the text and that re-reading is a purposeful activity which will help them to clarify their own responses.
- Ask students to be selective about the quotes so that they focus on the essential parts of the description. This can help later with choosing quotes as evidence for coursework.
- Similarly, students will need to be succinct with the detail they use in the thought-bubble as they consider the doctor's situation.

The Woman in Black

Use page 53 of this book to gain an insight into the physical description of the mysterious woman in the black veil.

This exercise is designed to assist students to get as clear a view as possible of the deliberately vague description of the woman. The students are given the text in enlarged form to assist close reading.

- The re-reading exercises can be done within the pairs, individually or as a whole class depending on the confidence of the readers.
- Once students have identified the phrases which give the passage its air of mystery, some discussion might ensue exploring the linguistic features of these descriptions, for example, the use of alliteration.

Clues in Context

Use page 54 of this book to begin some active and close inferential reading on selected extracts from the text.

The process of moving from active engagement with text to a reflective consideration of meaning is often a big jump for students. On this page, they are asked to make the text into a script, use it as such and then interrogate the same passage with a particular purpose. It is a staged development leading to thought-provoking activities.

- Organise the composition of groups so that the social mix is as constructive as possible.
- The initial active reading may require careful explanation and demonstration before students begin on their own.
- There is an example completed for students but some may need extra support in identifying the 'mysterious' phrases.
- Similarly, the final activity may need to be teacher-led with some groups who may not have the necessary skills to infer meaning from their choice of lines.

The Doctor's Fears

Use page 55 of this book in conjunction with the previous exercise to compare the group's predictions to the doctor's.

The doctor assists the reader at this point in the story by reflecting on the evidence revealed by the woman in the black veil. In doing so, he is neatly summarising and speculating on the evidence available to us as readers.

- Again, various methods of re-reading can be adopted. Choral reading with a figure representing the doctor surrounded by 'voices' in his head or simply teacher reading and emphasising the main points.
- By working in pairs to locate the doctor's three different rationales, students are given the security to attempt the exercise.
- Using students' own words to re-write the doctor's opinions will help to fix an understanding of his thinking in their minds.

THE BLACK VEIL

By Charles Dickens

A Walk on the Wild Side of Walworth

Use page 56 of this book to allow students to interpret text for themselves in illustrative form.

The link between words, pictures and understanding is an enigmatic triangular relationship. It does, however, regularly produce startling responses and insights from students. Drawing or art work as response to literature provides a valuable starting point for a discussion of the reader's response.

- Use the descriptions of Walworth on the left of the page as a stimulus for students' drawing. It may well be worthwhile reading the whole passage to them as they are quietly drawing.
- When complete, ask students about their diagrams and what they saw in the text.
- These responses can obviously be used for display either as original drafts or as fully completed pieces done for homework.

A Morality Tale

Use page 58 of this book to involve students in a creative written response to the story.

If students have completed the exercise on page 57, they will have a neat structure of ten summary points to begin this exercise. Re-telling stories in a different genre for a different audience is a valid way of assessing understanding within a more productive setting.

- Re-read the final two passages to students as an alternative to students reading it themselves. This will allow you to emphasise the moralistic tone of these passages.
- Explain the needs of younger readers in terms of simplicity, word choice, length and impact. Perhaps illustrations could be suggested as part of a longer project?
- A beginning to the story has been suggested, although it is not necessary to adopt this.

Playing Hangman

Use page 57 of this book to provide students with a ten-point summary of the story.

For students to begin to use the structure of the story to respond to in writing, or as a means of comparison with other stories, they will require an overview of the essential elements of the plot. This exercise combines a powerful image from the story, a summary exercise and a suggestion for a game with which most of them will be familiar.

- Brainstorming the elements of the story can be done as a whole class exercise or in pairs/groups depending on the requirements of the group at the time.
- The process of prioritising the essential ten events, or re-wording their work so that they combine points to make ten, will involve students in skills of summary and note-taking.
- The exercise is essentially a game and could be done as a timed activity to introduce an element of competition or as a collaborative, whole group exercise where consensus is required for the final choice of ten events.

Making Comparisons

Use page 59 of this book to begin the process of comparing and planning for a coursework assignment.

This story provides many possible points of comparison for a wider reading assignment. This page concentrates on three and provides a skeletal structure to assist planning. Students will obviously require assistance in choosing their other text and on deciding their point of comparison.

- Discuss their other text with students before deciding on the most appropriate point of comparison.
- Direct students to the most appropriate title and ask them to read their other text with that point in mind. They may wish to take notes as they read rather than when they have finished.
- The next stage will obviously involve:
  - selection of appropriate quotes and references to support their ideas
  - a planned structure for their assignment
  - an indication of how they will link these ideas into a coherent framework
  - drafted and re-drafted versions.

THE BLACK VEIL

By Charles Dickens

The Lonely Doctor

There is a classic beginning to this story. A lonely character sits by a fire with a storm raging outside. As readers, we need to be able to picture the scene and to understand a little of the background to the main character. To help you do this, a picture of the opening scene has been drawn for you.

Working in pairs:

① Read together the opening paragraph of the story.

② Look carefully at the drawing on this page. What sentences or phrases in this opening section can you see in the picture? Write these lines onto the page so that you are labelling the picture.

③ The doctor (or medical practitioner) is dreaming by the fire. In the space provided and working from the text, write what he is dreaming about.

THE BLACK VEIL

By Charles Dickens

The Woman in Black

It was a singularly tall woman, dressed in deep mourning, and standing so close to the door that her face almost touched the glass. The upper part of her figure was carefully muffled in a black shawl, as if for the purpose of concealment; and her face was shrouded by a thick black veil. She stood perfectly erect; her figure was drawn up to its full height, and though the surgeon felt that the eyes beneath the veil were fixed on him, she stood perfectly motionless, and evinced, by no gesture whatever, the slightest consciousness of his having turned towards her ...

... The surgeon drew a chair to the fire, and motioned the visitor to a seat. The mysterious figure slowly moved towards it. As the blaze shone upon the black dress, the surgeon observed that the bottom of it was saturated with mud and rain.

The woman who enters the doctor's surgery is dark and mysterious. Dickens deliberately creates a mysterious air about her through his description.

Working in pairs or on your own:

① Re-read the extracts describing the woman on this page.

② Find and underline the descriptions of the woman which make her sound mysterious.

③ Transfer them to this sheet so that you have a permanent record.

-
-
-
-
-
-

THE BLACK VEIL

By Charles Dickens

Clues in Context

Much of the mystery in this story comes about because Dickens, the writer, only *suggests* what is really happening. He uses conversations between the characters to drop hints about the real situation. This makes us, as readers, guess at the actual meaning of what is said.

Working in groups of three:

① Find and mark with a pencil from '"You are very wet," he said,' to 'The woman wept bitterly as she replied, "I could not."'

② Choose one person to read the doctor's dialogue, one to read the woman's and a third to read any other pieces.

③ In pencil, mark where the doctor speaks (D), where the woman speaks (W) and where the narrator speaks (N). Read aloud the conversation using as much expression as you can.

④ Go back over the extract and mark in pencil any lines which are mysterious in some way.

⑤ Complete the table at the bottom of this page. In the left hand column, jot down your mysterious lines and in the right hand column try to explain what they might mean. One has been completed for you.

Mysterious lines	Why is it mysterious?
'It is not for myself that I come to you.'	Why would she go to a doctor if it was for someone else?

THE BLACK VEIL

By Charles Dickens

The Doctor's Fears

It will be readily believed that so extraordinary a visit produced a considerable impression on the mind of the young surgeon; and that he speculated a great deal, and to very little purpose, on the possible circumstances of the case. In common with the generality of people, he had often heard and read of singular instances, in which a presentiment of death, at a particular day, or even minute, had been entertained and realised. At one moment, he was inclined to think that the present might be such a case; but then it occurred to him that all the anecdotes of the kind he had ever heard were of persons who had been troubled with a foreboding of their own death. This woman, however, spoke of another person – a man; and it was impossible to suppose that a mere dream or delusion of fancy would induce her to speak of his approaching dissolution with such terrible certainty as she had spoken. It could not be that the man was to be murdered in the morning, and that the woman, originally a consenting party, and bound to secrecy by an oath, had relented, and though unable to prevent the commission of some outrage on the victim, had determined to prevent his death, if possible, by the timely interposition of medical aid? The idea of such things happening within two miles of the metropolis appeared too wild and preposterous to be entertained beyond the instant. Then his original impression, that the woman's intellects were disordered, recurred; and, as it was the only mode of solving the difficulty with any degree of satisfaction, he obstinately made up his mind to believe that she was mad. Certain misgivings upon this point, however, stole upon his thoughts at the time, and presented themselves again and again through the long, dull course of a sleepless night; during which, in spite of all his efforts to the contrary, he was unable to banish the black veil from his disturbed imagination.

By this stage in the story, the doctor's mind is racing as he frantically tries to piece together the mystery of the person in the black veil.

Working in pairs:

① Carefully re-read the extract on this page.

② As you read it, try to find the three different interpretations which the doctor thinks would explain the woman's story.

③ In the space provided on this page, write out three interpretations in your own words.

-
-
-

THE BLACK VEIL

By Charles Dickens

A Walk on the Wild Side of Walworth

Walworth is described as a bleak and dangerous place by Dickens. However, you are now an experienced reader who is able to use text to make your own mental picture.

Working on your own:

① Use the descriptions of Walworth from the story to imagine what it must have looked like.

② In the four picture frames below, draw what you think the places looked like.

1 ... now and then a miserable patch of garden ground with a few old boards knocked together for a summer house.

2 Occasionally, a filthy-looking woman would make her appearance from the door of a dirty house to empty the contents of some cooking utensil into the gutter in front, or to scream after a little slipshod girl who had contrived to stagger a few yards from the door under the weight of a sallow infant almost as big as herself.

3 It was a small, low building, one story above the ground, with even a more desolate and unpromising exterior than any he had yet passed. An old, yellow curtain was closely drawn across the window upstairs, and the parlour shutters were closed but not fastened. The house was detached from any other, and, as it stood at an angle of a narrow lane, there was no other habitation in sight.

4 It was a little cold room ... the unwholesome moisture was stealing down the walls in long slug-like tracks.

1	2
3	**4**

THE BLACK VEIL

By Charles Dickens

Playing Hangman

This page is designed to help you put together the main elements of the story.
Working in pairs or small groups:

① Brainstorm all of the events which take place in the story.

② Decide on the most important ten.

③ Number these and write them onto the 'hangman' diagram below.

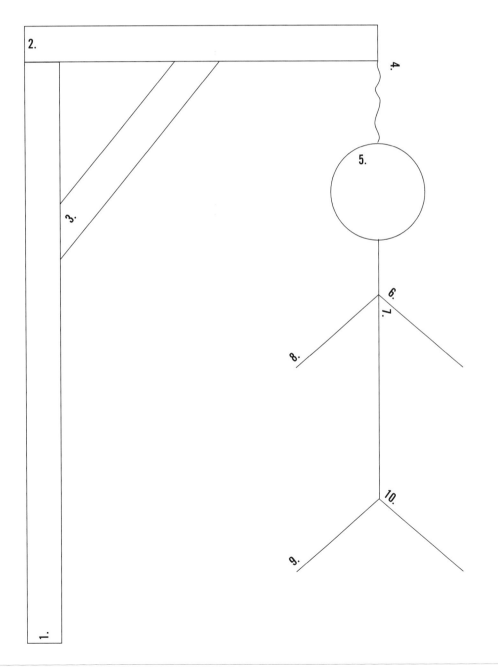

THE BLACK VEIL

By Charles Dickens

A Morality Tale

Although this is a mystery story, the final two paragraphs are not mysterious at all. In these, Dickens gives the reader a brief history of the woman, her son and the success the doctor achieves in later life.

Dickens seems to suggest that because the doctor was so kind to the woman, he was blessed and achieved riches because of his good deeds.

Working on your own:

① Read the final two paragraphs of the story again.

② Imagine that you have decided to write a letter to *The Times* newspaper about your concern for the conditions of the poor in London.

③ You could choose as your subject the poverty-stricken conditions of the people south of the Thames, the over use of hanging as a form of punishment or the lack of support for people in genuine distress.

④ Use the space on this page to begin drafting the letter. You will need to decide on a suitable address for yourself. The first part of the letter has been completed for you.

The Editor,
The Times Newspaper,
Fleet Street,
London.

23rd November, 1862

Dear Sir,

I wish to express my grave concern over...

THE BLACK VEIL

By Charles Dickens

Making Comparisons

The Black Veil is both a mystery and a horror story. There are a number of essential ways in which it can be compared to another text of your choice.

① Look at the ideas in the left hand column of the table and decide which you will use.

② Read your alternative text and jot down the equivalent notes so that you have a starting point for your comparison.

The Black Veil	Other Text
1. Compare the way Dickens has created a mood of mystery with a similar story you have chosen. ● he uses a stormy, dark night ● he includes a surprise visitor ● he describes a mysterious figure ● he keeps hinting at the full story but only reveals it at the end	
2. Compare the central mysterious figure with another character from a different story. ● the woman arrives and behaves in a frightened way ● she is dressed in a way which creates curiosity ● she only hints at the story she has to tell ● she speaks in riddles	
3. Compare the setting in Walworth with another setting from a story you choose. ● it is well away from civilised society ● it is inhabited by harsh, poverty-stricken people ● the buildings are dilapidated ● the writer suggests that criminals live there	

THE MELANCHOLY HUSSAR

By Thomas Hardy

Stimulus Page

Use the stimulus page in the Student's Anthology to begin to stimulate interest in, and curiosity about *The Melancholy Hussar* prior to reading.

Two of the boxes suggest storytelling activities. These could be organised in a variety of ways: collecting ideas for homework, telling the story for the first time to a partner in pairs, then refining it and relating it to a larger group. First ideas, or the final version, could be written.

Predictions

Use page 63 of this book for this activity. Stop at the points indicated by the TB 63 icons at the side of the story, and discuss and then note down ideas about what might happen next, and why.

There are several possible stopping places, but the icons mark three significant points in the story. Make students question key sentences: Why are the York Hussars mentioned? What might follow Phyllis's decision to run away with the Hussar? What might be the real reason for Humphrey's visit? The students will also need to justify their ideas as they do this activity.

- Each time you pause in the reading, ask the students to predict what might happen next. Encourage them to go beyond wild guesses, by encouraging them to think back and look for clues, and also to consider the common structures and plots of other stories they have read.
- their initial ideas could be shared with the person sitting next to them – to encourage the participation of everyone – before hearing ideas expressed to the whole group.
- at the second or final stopping point, students could be asked to note down their ideas immediately onto the sheet, so that they can compare the responses later. For this activity there will need to be no conferring!

The Heart of Phyllis Grove

Page 64 of this book enables students to focus at certain points on the feelings of Phyllis towards the two men in her life.

This activity highlights the very different feelings Phyllis has for Humphrey and then for Matthäus. These are quite precisely described by Hardy, and a study of them helps students to an understanding of Phyllis's circumstances and her expectations and dreams. This can be used, therefore, as one of the first steps to a grasp of Hardy's themes and concerns.

- Emphasise that this activity is about the feelings Phyllis has for the two men, not the writer's attitude to them.
- Stop at the places indicated by the symbol to focus on the parts of the text that describe her thoughts and feelings about marriage and love.
- The students will need to use their own words to explain what they believe she feels, and choose important quotes for the boxes at the bottom of the page.

Four Characters

Page 65 of this book enables students to begin to study character by making notes on each of the main characters as they are revealed.

The study of these four people also sheds light on the particular situation of Phyllis; she is seen to be influenced by three very different men whose characteristics are vividly described by Hardy. Again, this is a page which could be used as the reading progresses, with observations being noted down at intervals.

- Decide where to stop, or use this page after reading the whole text. The pauses to make predictions could also be used as an opportunity to study character.
- Students often need help when they are choosing words and phrases to describe a person's character. They will need to be encouraged to focus on personality – what someone is like – not their appearance or their actions. Examples such as the ones on the left can be a helpful prompt.
- Note-taking is also a skill that students need to practise. In pairs, ask the students to tell their partner what they feel one of the characters is like. The partner listens, and then writes down the main points only of what was said. The pair then discuss the notes to see if they can be reduced further, and to check for sense and appropriateness.

THE MELANCHOLY HUSSAR

By Thomas Hardy

To My Dear Mother

On page 66 of the book students create the letter Matthäus writes to his mother, as he plans his escape.

This piece of imaginative writing enables students to consider the plans, feelings and dreams of Matthäus, and to think about the appropriate style and layout to use for the letter. It is important to develop this activity by asking students to consider how to portray the character of Matthäus, how to reveal his personal thoughts, how to organise the content in order to gain a sympathetic response from the reader.

- Remind students of the possible layout of a letter. One possible example is given on the photocopiable sheet. Ask them to think about the arrangement of the address, opening, paragraphs and the close of the letter, by filling in the spaces on the sample format.
- Notes will then be needed, so that all necessary information is included, both to make the writing convincing and to help students to show their understanding of the character. Groups could gather the relevant facts from the text, taking a couple of paragraphs each, and arranging all the details they feel are significant onto a piece of sugar paper.
- The use of language needs to be discussed, so that appropriate phrases are incorporated, and so that the historical aspects are considered. Ask students to make a collection of words and phrases from the actual text that are examples of the language (in English, of course!) Matthäus would use.

Metaphors

Use the examples given on page 67 of this book to explore Hardy's use of metaphor to explain Phyllis's situation and feelings about her life.

This activity acts as a study of a specific technique, as well as providing students with a way to examine the isolation and restrictions of Phyllis's life. As the phrases themselves are quite complex, it would be better to organise the class into small, mixed groups to do the activity. This task can be done as the reading is progressing, or after the story has been finished.

- Revise 'metaphor', with easy examples, given to, or collected from, the class.
- Find the examples given on the sheet in the text itself

– see TB 67 icons at the side. Ask each group to read around the quote to find the context and remind themselves of the point in the story.

- The advice to the groups needs to include the use of dictionaries, but also the possibility of there being various shades of meaning for each metaphor – that their personal responses have validity.
- Ask each group to focus on Phyllis: her life, her situation, the confines of an isolated existence. What effect does this have on her?

Decisions

Page 68 of this book provides a drama activity that explores the conflicting voices inside Phyllis's head as she makes the two major decisions of the story.

This activity uses the ideas of a drama technique sometimes known as 'Conscience Alley', where individuals use their voices on both sides of the person in role, in order to make the conflicting ideas concrete. As the pressure builds, the central figure ends the activity by interrupting the voices with the expression of the final decision.

- Some warm-up activity often helps here, so the pair work is an important stage.
- Encouragement to use varied tones and volume, as well as simple movements or positions, could be given by questioning, as each group is visited.
- The activity works best if it is not over-rehearsed. Groups should be encouraged to let the drama run without interruption and planning, before they break off to reflect on what they have created.
- The final task could be a whole class activity where each group presents their version. The discussion following this would need to summarise the difficulty of these decisions, and begin to examine the reasons behind them.

THE MELANCHOLY HUSSAR

By Thomas Hardy

Making Comparisons 1

Page 69 of this book helps students compare the two stories in the anthology by Thomas Hardy, and then to move on to another writer.

This page offers a 'writing frame' to help students focus on particular aspects of two stories by the same writer. The work gives a clearer view of a writer's concerns and techniques, and helps the students to appreciate his particular style and preoccupations. It could usefully be used as a basis for a study of one of Hardy's novels, or as preliminary work to an assignment comparing different writers.

- After reading both stories, ask students to jot down the main points about the setting, then characters, plot and themes. The column on the right completes the activity by asking the students to decide whether the two stories are very similar — tick — or very different — cross.
- The themes section may be more difficult, so preliminary ideas could be written on the back of the sheet, perhaps after conferring in pairs, and then discussing their findings as a whole class, before filling in the actual box.

Making Comparisons 2

Page 70 of this book enables students to study an example of a paragraph taken from a literary essay, as a guide to writing more successful paragraphs.

As the students begin to draft assignments, they often find creating paragraphs difficult. This sheet offers a way for them to stop and study the way sentences can be linked and developed, and ideas explained more fully.

Possible titles for comparative essays include:

- Write about a character from each of the texts. Do you notice any similarities between them?
- What do you think Hardy was really interested in and wanted to share with his readers? What did you learn about the writer of the other text you studied?
- Choose an aspect of the stories that you found interesting or successful. This could be pieces of description, or characters, points of suspense or fear, or themes and ideas. Write about each story, explaining what you have chosen, and saying why it meant something to you.

THE MELANCHOLY HUSSAR

By Thomas Hardy

Predictions

Possibilities	Why do you think this?
1. '… aforesaid York Hussars.'	
2. '… by her confidence in him.'	
3. … 'help me out of a mighty difficulty.'	

THE MELANCHOLY HUSSAR

By Thomas Hardy

The Heart of Phyllis Grove

What are Phyllis's feelings for the men she meets? Explain them in your own words when you have looked again at the key sections of the story.

Humphrey Gould   Matthäus Tina

Key Quotes

THE MELANCHOLY HUSSAR

By Thomas Hardy

The Four Characters

Think about:

- personalities
- what the person is like
- their attitudes
- their manner
- what their behaviour reveals about them
- what their interests or habits are

Use:

- a variety of words and phrases
- a formal style of language – no slang!
- a thesaurus – to find the best words!

Phyllis	Her Father
Humphrey	**Matthäus**

THE MELANCHOLY HUSSAR

By Thomas Hardy

To My Dear Mother

Imagine you are Matthäus, writing the letter home to his mother. For the purpose of this activity, you will need to write in English!

① Remind yourself of the layout of a letter. There are several acceptable formats, but the one shown here is commonly used in handwritten letters. What goes on in each of the positions indicated? Put your answers at the end of the lines given.

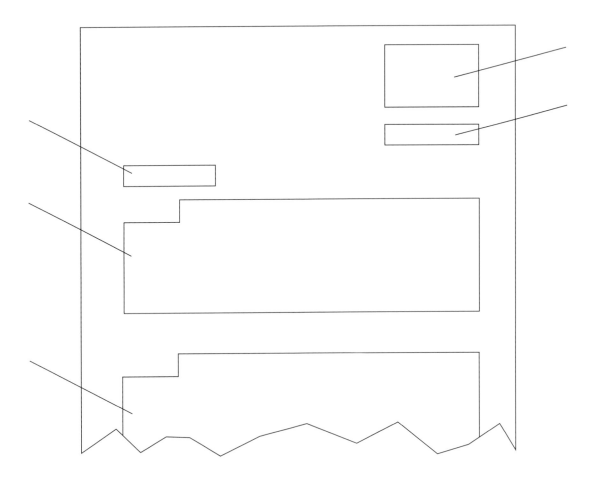

② Then collect a list of things to include in your letter. Consider: events, plans, thoughts, feelings.

③ Now think about the type of words and phrases it would be best to use. Remember! Nineteenth-century words. Use the text of the story to help you.

THE MELANCHOLY HUSSAR

By Thomas Hardy

Metaphors

> '... her social condition was twilight ...'

> '... the (golden radiance) of the ... York Hussars.' ...

> 'The stone wall of necessity ...'

> 'The house ... was a prison to Phyllis'

① In your small groups discuss what you feel each of these phrases means, and then fill
   in the boxes. Find two other metaphors, and do the same with them.

THE MELANCHOLY HUSSAR

By Thomas Hardy

Decisions

There are two points in the story where Phyllis must make a major decision. One, whether to run away with Matthäus, and the other whether to return to Humphrey. Each can be explored using drama.

① Find the place in the text where Phyllis is debating whether to run away — TB 68. Remind yourself of this section of the story.

② Turn to the person next to you, and tell each other what you think is going through her mind. Try to find as many reasons for and against going as possible. You could jot these down if you wish.

③ Now gather together in groups of about five or seven. One of you will need to represent Phyllis, and stand in the middle. The others arrange themselves on opposite sides, to represent the opposing ideas in her mind. One side will be telling her to go with Matthäus, and why, and the other will be telling her she must stay.

④ As you voice these thoughts, think about creating a sense of pressure, a feeling of her conscience battling against other hopes and desires. How might you create this?

⑤ The person in the role of Phyllis ends the drama by interrupting the voices, and stating her final decision.

⑥ You will need to practise and refine this, before presenting it to the rest of the class.

⑦ Now, do the same with the second decision, working from instruction number 3. Are the conflicting voices saying similar or different things?

THE MELANCHOLY HUSSAR

By Thomas Hardy

Making Comparisons 1

Use this table to compare two stories by Thomas Hardy.

	The Melancholy Hussar	The Withered Arm	√ or ✕
Setting			
Characters			
Plot			
Themes			

Now do a similar exercise using a text by a different author.
What do you notice is different about their preoccupations and the way they construct their stories?

THE MELANCHOLY HUSSAR

By Thomas Hardy

Making Comparisons 2

Creating Paragraphs

Hardy's main character, Phyllis Grove, is a lonely young woman, cut off from the community. This isolation means that she has no friends in whom to confide, and she therefore makes her decisions alone, without guidance. Similarly, D. H. Lawrence's heroine in *The Horse Dealer's Daughter* is an isolated female character, having few choices, and little opportunity to talk and share …

Highlight the words or phrases you feel are useful in this example of a paragraph. Can you see how the writer develops the point she is making?

Now try to write your own analysis of a particular point you wish to make about the texts you are studying.

THE YELLOW WALLPAPER

By Charlotte Perkins Gilman

Stimulus Page

Use the stimulus page in the Student's Anthology to begin to stimulate interest in, and curiosity about *The Yellow Wallpaper* prior to reading.

A Perfect Match?

Use page 73 of this book to reflect upon the language of benevolent repression used by the husband, John.

Throughout the story, the narrator's husband (the doctor, John) seems to have an unhealthy control over his wife's actions and even her thoughts and feelings. An understanding of their relationship is central to an appreciation of the narrator's dilemma and her eventual obsession with the wallpaper.

- Most of the quotes have already been chosen for students to consider. Paired discussion is suggested initially to allow for tentative exploration of the language of their relationship.
- It is really the difference between what is actually said and the sub-text of those remarks which will provide insights for students. Stress the importance of the effect the statements are having on the wife as students complete the negative column.
- Some plenary discussion may help to consolidate the groups' understanding of the relationship before moving onto the remainder of the story.

The Secret Diary

Use page 74 of this book to summarise the story in seven, brief diary entries.

This story is written as a diary in seven sections. As such, it makes sense to ask students to use the same genre to encapsulate the essence of what is gradually being revealed. The diary form is a subtle process which constantly asks the reader to delve beyond what the character is saying and to question and interpret comments for him or herself. This 'writing-in-role' allows students to adopt this persona and to practise the subtlety it demands.

- Working in pairs will allow students to experiment with the 'voice' of the character in an interactive situation.
- The Student Anthology is marked with icons to guide the reading of the class. It is a convenient way of providing markers. Students should read to each stop, discuss and summarise.

TB 74

- Ensure that all pairs have completed the summary by sharing what students have written. This will provide a framework for studying the story as a whole and the issues and themes which emerge.

Other Voices

Use page 75 of this book to dramatise the relationship between the narrator, her husband, John, and sister, Jennie.

The relationship between the narrator and her husband is the essence of the story. Enactment will allow opportunities for students to fully appreciate and explore the dynamics of this relationship. The intention of this page is to focus students' attention on the way in which the repeated use of a patronising tone can be used as a tool of repression.

- Small group improvisation is very effective with experienced students. With less-experienced classes, you might need to choose two volunteers plus yourself as teacher-in-role to provide a model of the way to proceed.
- Groups of at least three are essential to this exercise but an alternative would be to use a fourth group member to act as a non-participating observer who reports back to the group on how they used their body language and tone of voice during the re-enactment.
- Use the statements in the wife's thought bubble as starters. Groups may wish to select their own moments from the story to enact depending on the path of the discussion.

Barred Windows

Use page 76 of this book to collect words and phrases to do with repression and imprisonment.

This page can be used concurrent with reading or as an exercise at the conclusion of the story. The language of patronising repression becomes more obvious when it is collected and compiled in a format which emphasises its effect.

- Encourage students to interrogate the text by skim reading and locating the essential comments.
- Compare the selections of the various groups at the end of the exercise through discussion of choices and the effects of the language.
- This collection of quotes can be used for display purposes and as an aide memoire for the Making Comparisons sheet on page 80.

THE YELLOW WALLPAPER

By Charlotte Perkins Gilman

The Wallpaper

Use page 77 of this book to link descriptions of the wallpaper in the text with the state of mind of the narrator.

The process by which the narrator and the wallpaper seem to interact, leading to the malevolent personification of the wallpaper, is one which the reader needs to track in order to make sense of the conclusion. This page also provides an opportunity for students to use information retrieval skills and to reflect on their selections.

- This is a small group exercise because the process of skimming and locating can be shared and the final selection agreed and discussed within the group.
- Ask students to mark in pencil all references to the wallpaper in the text. There are too many for inclusion on this page, so a process of selection will be necessary to prioritise.
- Students may require further discussion and explanation before they are ready to attempt this activity. Extrapolating from wallpaper patterns to states of madness is a sophisticated leap but once this 'reading' is explained, students will have the tools to make their own diagnosis.

Interpretations 1

Use page 78 of this book to help students make sense of the conclusion to the story.

The final paragraphs of *The Yellow Wallpaper* are baffling and surreal. The ending is open to interpretation and any reading of it is dependent upon an understanding of the themes already explored. This page can be used in conjunction with page 79.

- Readings of the final section can be varied to suit the needs of the group: individually and silently, by the teacher to the group or chorally with students taking an active role.
- Ask students to record their first impressions of what has happened without discussion. This should help to spice up the discussion afterwards if people have different viewpoints to defend.
- Handling the final discussion will depend on the variety of interpretations. Perhaps students could be asked to compose a brief 'write-on' as a way of defining their own ending?

Interpretations 2

Use page 79 of this book to stimulate further discussion on the possible meanings behind the story.

This page contains six statements representing various 'psychological' interpretations for the story's outcome. There is space for students to add their own statements because, no doubt, there will be other interpretations.

- Work in groups large enough to allow discussion.
- The placing of the statements on the continuum can be done in groups or as a whole class exercise with groups giving their reasons.
- Encourage groups to complete the four blank statements. Use these to broaden discussion as a prelude to the written responses on page 78.

Making Comparisons

Use page 80 of this book to plan a coursework piece comparing *The Yellow Wallpaper* with another text.

The comparative assignment is now a major piece of coursework for all examination syllabuses at Key Stage 4. This page provides a number of opportunities for students to consider points of comparison and to begin the process of structuring an answer.

- Rather than deal with differences and similarities, students are asked to focus simply on aspects of sameness.
- Selecting one character from both texts and concentrating on feelings, attitudes and states of mind provides another simple focus for a comparative question.
- *The Yellow Wallpaper* takes the plight of women as one of its central themes. Students may need to back-up their planning with some discussion of feminism and Charlotte Gilman's place in the emergence of women writers.

THE YELLOW WALLPAPER

By Charlotte Perkins Gilman

A Perfect Match?

Relationships between two people can be destructive even when both parties are wanting the best for each other. In *The Yellow Wallpaper* the husband seems to be trying very hard to make his wife's life as comfortable and trouble-free as possible. Is he trying too hard? What effect is he really having on her?

In pairs:

① Analyse their relationship by looking closely at some of the comments (and directions) given by the husband.

② Discuss what he says in the left hand column and, in the Negatives column, write down what you think is the actual effect of his words. (One example has been completed for you.)

③ Still working in pairs, try to find other comments made by the husband which, although apparently helpful, actually have a damaging effect on his wife.

Positives	Negatives
(John is) very careful and loving, and hardly lets me stir without special direction	John is too much in control and he is making her more nervous
(John) scoffs openly at any talk of things not to be felt and seen and put down in figures	
(John says) there is really nothing the matter with one but temporary nervous depression – a slight hysterical tendency	
I am absolutely forbidden to 'work' until I am well again	
John says the very worst thing I can do is think about my condition	
We took the nursery at the top of the house	

THE YELLOW WALLPAPER

By Charlotte Perkins Gilman

The Secret Diary

This story appears as seven entries into a diary by the narrator. As you read through the story, use the appropriate space below to summarise each entry.

You may wish to work on your own or in pairs for this exercise.

① Read through the story up to the point where you see a **TB 74**. Stop reading and, as briefly as you can, summarise the events in the space provided.

② Read on until the next **TB 74** and record your summary.

③ Repeat this until you have a full record of the story.

1.

2.

3.

4.

5.

6.

7.

THE YELLOW WALLPAPER

By Charlotte Perkins Gilman

Other Voices

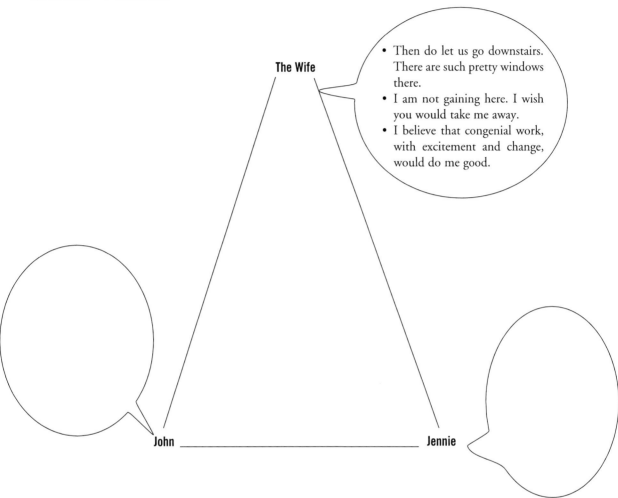

The Wife

• Then do let us go downstairs. There are such pretty windows there.
• I am not gaining here. I wish you would take me away.
• I believe that congenial work, with excitement and change, would do me good.

John _____ Jennie

One way to begin to realise the sort of subtle pressure the wife is under is to use drama to explore it.

Work in groups of three. Either sit at your desks or move into a suitable space.

① The wife has three statements in her thought bubble. Each of these can be used to begin a short piece of improvised drama.

② Choose who will be the wife, John, the husband, and Jennie, the sister-in-law.

③ Begin the improvisation by using one of the wife's statements. It is the job of the other two characters to persuade her – gently but firmly – that she is wrong.

④ When you have finished, discuss whether you think the husband and his sister were really helping. How could they have done things differently?

THE YELLOW WALLPAPER

By Charlotte Perkins Gilman

Barred Windows

The narrator who tells us this story constantly uses the language of imprisonment to describe her dilemma.

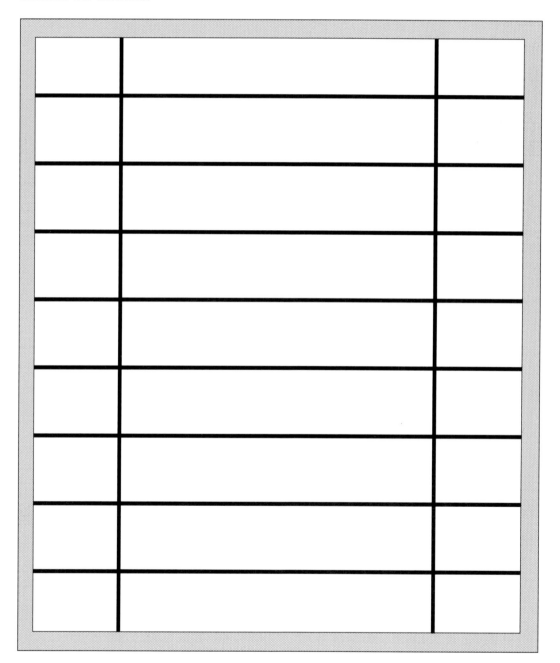

Working in groups of three or four:

① Use the space in between the bars to compile your own list of words and phrases which suggest imprisonment.

② Keep this sheet, or display it for future reference.

THE YELLOW WALLPAPER

By Charlotte Perkins Gilman

The Wallpaper

In the nursery, the narrator becomes darkly fascinated by the wallpaper which she is forced to stare at day after day. Her descriptions of it are vivid and intense but they also give us clues about her state of mind.

Working in small groups:

① Skim read the story and find any references to the wallpaper – its shapes, colours, patterns, and movements. Mark them with a pencil.

② Number what you consider to be the 12 most important of these passages.

③ Write the quotes into the table and briefly summarise what you feel was the narrator's state of mind at the time. One is done for you.

Quote	State of mind
'It makes me tired to follow it. I will take a nap I guess.'	The wallpaper seems to be mesmerising her, as if it could hypnotise. Her tiredness could be a kind of breakdown coming on.

THE YELLOW WALLPAPER

By Charlotte Perkins Gilman

Interpretations 1

But here I can creep smoothly on the floor, and my shoulder just fits in that long smooch around the wall, so I cannot lose my way.

Why, there's John at the door!

It is no use, young man, you can't open it!

How he does call and pound!

Now he's crying to Jennie for an axe.

It would be a shame to break down that beautiful door!

'John, dear!' said I in the gentlest voice. 'The key is down by the front steps, under a plantain leaf!'

That silenced him for a few moments.

Then he said, very quietly indeed, 'Open the door, my darling!'

'I can't,' said I. 'The key is down by the front door under a plantain leaf!' And then I said it again, several times, very gently and slowly, and said it so often that he had to go and see, and he got it of course, and came in. He stopped short by the door.

'What is the matter?' he cried. 'For God's sake, what are you doing!'

I kept on creeping just the same, but I looked at him over my shoulder.

'I've got out at last,' said I, 'in spite of you and Jane. And I've pulled off most of the paper, so you can't put me back!'

Now why should that man have fainted? But he did, and right across my path by the wall, so that I had to creep over him every time!

The ending of this story is quite bizarre and it asks you, as a reader, to decide for yourself what is happening.

Work in pairs or small groups.

① Re-read the final section of the story.

② In the space around the extract, jot down your initial ideas about what might have happened and what it might mean.

③ Now, consider the story as a whole. What are the possible interpretations? Use sheet 2 on page 79 to help you.

Evidence	Interpretations

THE YELLOW WALLPAPER

By Charlotte Perkins Gilman

Interpretations 2

Strongly Disagree ━━━━━━━━━━━━━━━━━━━━━━━ **Strongly Agree**

To begin to fully appreciate this story, you will need to consider its themes including some theories of madness.

Work in groups of three or four, or as a whole class:

① Read each of the statements in turn.

② Discuss them and decide where you would place them on the continuum.

③ In the space provided, make up four theories of your own to explain her behaviour, write them down and discuss their position on the continuum.

Statements:

1. It was the husband's fault. He deliberately drove her to madness.

2. Her reactions are simply the result of post-natal depression.

3. should have been told to snap out of it and pull herself together.

4. Being unoccupied and made to rest is the main cause of her distress.

5. The husband, John, was simply a bit over-protective.

6. She's a creative person whose 'spark' is denied. This is what destroys her.

7.

8.

9.

10.

THE YELLOW WALLPAPER

By Charlotte Perkins Gilman

Making Comparisons

When you have chosen the text you wish to compare with *The Yellow Wallpaper*, make preliminary notes by answering the following questions:

① Briefly list all the similarities you notice between the two stories.

The Yellow Wallpaper	Other Text
•	•
•	•
•	•
•	•

② Choose one character from each text and compare them in terms of feelings, attitudes and states of mind.

The Yellow Wallpaper	Other Text
•	•
•	•
•	•
•	•

③ What does each story seem to be saying about women in the society of that time? At this time women were considered to be:

The Yellow Wallpaper	Other Text
•	•
•	•
•	•
•	•